LAMPI DI GE

Graphic design: Studio Link (www.studio-link.it)
Translation: Joshua Burkholder

www.editorialescienza.it
www.giunti.it

via Bolognese, 165 - 50139 Florence, Italy
via Beccaria, 6 - 34133 Trieste, Italy
First published: December 2012

Certificato PEFC

Questo prodotto è realizzato con materia prima da foreste gestite in maniera sostenibile e da fonti controllate

www.pefc.it

Printed in Italia by
Giunti Industrie Grafiche - Prato

Luca Novelli

Leonardo
and the Pen that Drew the Future

Content

Leonardo

A legend even in his own time, the figure of Leonardo da Vinci united both the arts and the sciences: on the one hand he was a painter and skilled draftsman, and on the other an inventor and tireless researcher. So wondrous were his talents that he was even accused of witchcraft, and many of his contemporaries saw him as some sort of wizard at the service of powerful nobles. Many of Leonardo's futuristic inventions are still with us today, including contact lenses and the armored vehicle.
He even devised a writing instrument that resembled the modern fountain pen: Leonardo's new contraption didn't require being dipped repeatedly into an inkwell, unlike the quill—the only tool for writing at the time.
In this book Leonardo himself tells us his life story, recounting all his adventures, disappointments, and successes.

WHAT YOU'LL FIND IN THIS BOOK

There's me, Leonardo, telling my story.

There's my childhood with my grandparents in a little town in the country.

There's my apprenticeship in Florence, in the great master Verrocchio's workshop.

There's my life and work as an engineer and architect in the service of the most powerful princes of the Renaissance.

There's the true story behind my best-known and most extraordinary works.

There are my scientific and technological practical jokes.

Lastly, there's a dictionary listing my most amazing discoveries and inventions.

LEONARDO'S WORLD 500 YEARS AGO

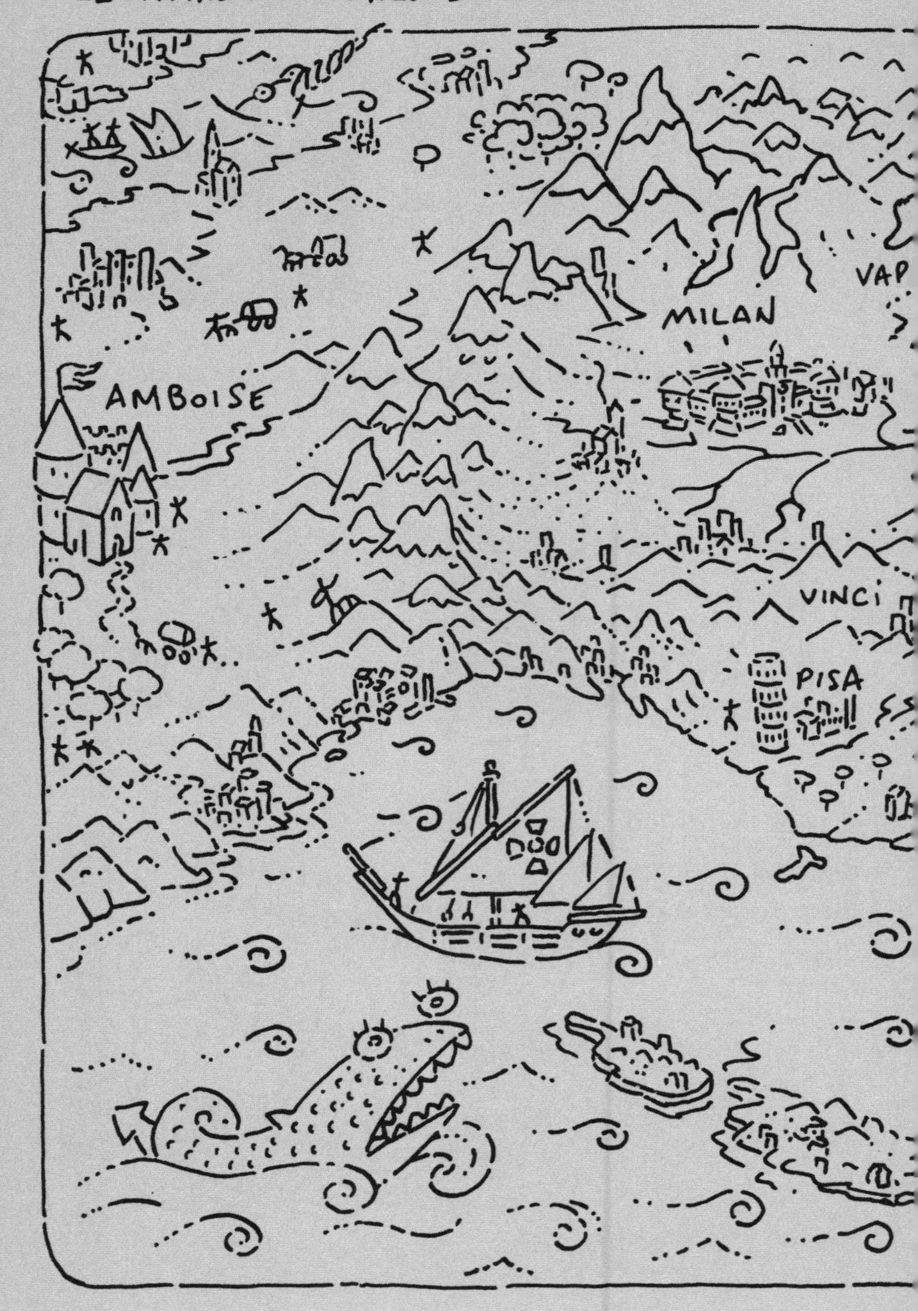

MUGHAL
EMPIRE
MANTUA
VENICE
RIMINI
FLORENCE
ROME
EDITERRANEAN
SEA

Leonardo was born forty years before Christopher Columbus reached the coasts of what would later come to be called America. He was born in a small town in the territory of Florence, which was at the time the capital of one of the many little states that Italy was divided into. Leonardo grew up at the end of the historical period of Europe known as the Middle Ages, a period in which the sciences and the arts were relatively overlooked. By the time he was an adult and had established himself as an artist and scientist, the era now known as the Renaissance had begun. Because of Leonardo's immense contribution to the culture of his day, many people think of him as the quintessential Renaissance man, the one who more than anyone else represents the renascence, or rebirth, of the arts, of science, and of reason over superstition.

1. Me, Leonardo

Welcome folks!
My name's Leonardo, I'm the son of the local notary, Piero da Vinci. I was born on the 15th day of April in the year 1452 in the village of Anchiano, a handful of houses close to Vinci. My mother gave birth to me on a Saturday. The time was "22:30," as you modern folks would say, with your fancy clocks and wristwatches. But what my grandpa Antonio wrote in his little book that day was that my birth came "in the third hour after nightfall". You see, he writes down absolutely everything, it's his job to record how many olives were picked, how much oil was extracted from them, how much grain was threshed…
and so he also noted the exact moment when I came into this world.
I was born in a modest country house owned by my father's family.

My mother's name is Caterina.
I remember her as being beautiful and sweet. But my father didn't marry her because she's a commoner, whereas he belongs to one of the most important families in Vinci.

This matter was rarely mentioned at home, especially after my dad Piero married Albiera, the daughter of a notary from Florence.

For her part, my mum Caterina ended up marrying a guy named Attaccabrighe, with whom she had five other children: four girls and a boy. She went to live in a tiny little house in a town nearby. Since I was sent to live with grandma and grandpa, I only saw her once: she had a bunch of kids hanging from her skirts. I remember that she smiled at me.

I like living with my grandparents: I don't go to school much, and have lots of free time. Grandpa Antonio has taught me to read, though. And when I write I use my left hand, because I'm left-handed.
I like exploring in the woods, either alone or with Uncle Francesco. He tells me incredible stories about the animals and plants in our area, and he's taught me how to cross streams and swamps safely.
I find water really fascinating, and have learned to respect it. I know what a tranquil river like the Arno can do when it gets upset. I've seen it sweep away everything: animals, people, and entire houses. Nothing could stop it. The sight of its anger will remain with me for the rest of my life.

The most common machines in use in Leonardo's day were water-powered mills.

Every village and every castle had a water-mill, usually built alongside a nearby stream. The waterwheel drove the machinery inside the mill for grinding wheat to make flour, and for pressing olives to extract their oil. In some regions water-mills were also used for producing paper, or for forging metals. Throughout his life, water and machines would fascinate Leonardo, and he went on to invent contraptions so ingenious that they would not actually be built until our own day and age.

During his own lifetime and for the next two centuries, the only sources of energy for powering machinery remained wind and water, in addition to the brute force of animals or humans.

2. Drawing is Fun!

Now I'm sitting with Uncle Francesco outside the tavern. He's something of a rascal. Grandpa Antonio says that uncle is only interested in girls, drinking, and eating. Still, he's very good to me. He's been teaching me how to draw with charcoal on paper.

For us, paper is quite a rare material. You won't find any paper in the houses of poor folk or peasants. They don't need it, since they don't have to read or write. But as my Dad is a notary, we've loads of paper, quills, and inkwells all over the house.

And not just paper: we even have a few books, which are very rare objects indeed. We actually call them “codices”, plural of the Latin word codex, and they are written by hand, like the big books you see in churches. Some of them are really beautiful, and have colorful figures illustrating the beginning of every chapter.

Grandpa says that nowadays books can be reproduced in many copies. This process, called printing, was invented by a man named Gutenberg in Mainz, Germany. But the technique won’t spread to my area for many years. News doesn’t travel as fast here as does in your era.

I often go to the pottery workshop, where I’ve learnt to shape clay and to mold vases, plates and small sculptures. Afterwards, the potter bakes them in type of oven called a kiln.

Sometimes during my explorations of the hills around Vinci I come across weird and wonderful things, like shells and the remains of strange little sea animals. My grandmothers says they were carried up here by the Great Flood… but I'm not so sure.
I must admit, my life here is pretty nice, but somehow the town seems to get smaller and smaller every day.
I wish I were a bird so I could fly. Actually I think that flying is in my future: when I was little I even dreamt of a giant bird called a kite that landed next to me.

Today my father came to Vinci to visit grandma and grandpa. He's an important guy. Although I'm his first-born son, I'm illegitimate. This means I won't be allowed to become a notary like him. That's how things work here in Florence. But who cares! Dad loves me, in his own way: he's come to take me with him.

When Leonardo first passed through its gates, Florence was one of the most lively and prosperous centers in Europe. The political stability of recent decades had led to extraordinary cultural and artistic boom. The dominant families were enlightened bankers and merchants. Within the walls were a thousand workshops and everywhere you looked some new building was under construction: a huge church, a convent, a hospital. With each visit, Leonardo would explore the city with the same curiosity that gripped him during his excursions in the hills around Vinci. The difference here was that Florence was full of pictures of things he had never seen before—stories of battles, of saints and great men of the past. Indeed, the painters and sculptors of the Renaissance had rediscovered the art of ancient Greece and Rome, and were recreating it with a new splendor.

3. Florence

Now I live in the city, in my father Ser Piero's house. You should see how the cooks and servants pamper me! My father works in politics and big business. He's gotten married again, and now I have enough half-brothers to field a football team. He sends me to abacus school, where they teach you to count on this clever wooden frame with sliding beads. It's a kind of calculator, and is essential for business in a city of merchants like Florence. The headmaster says that I am a good learner, but a bit odd. Luckily, he hasn't forced me to use my right hand. Some of the more severe teachers try to "correct" left-handed students by smacking them with a rod. That's crazy! You cannot correct Nature, you should help it. In any case, I draw pretty well with my left hand. Even my dad says so.

Today is a decisive day in my life. My father has gathered up my drawings and brought me to the most busy art workshop in the city, run by a guy called Andrea del Verrocchio.

Master Verrocchio is a renowned artist, but also a shrewd businessman.

His workshop resembles the kind of studio that important designers in your day have. It is full of people busy doing something—designers, draftsmen, illustrators, guys drawing diagrams or building scale models. Here they make everything from jewels and statues to interior decoration and stage scenery. Sometimes you create something yourself, at other times you follow the design of someone else: it all makes practice. Verrocchio himself is an engineer as well as an amazing painter, but he doesn't mind making banners and stuff for celebrations and processions, or even funerals.

There are several other young guys working in the shop, each one with big ambitions. Two of these will become really big names in future: Sandro Botticelli and Pietro Vannucci, better known as Perugino.

My first job will be to grind down certain types of mineral to extract their pigment. But my workmate Botticelli assures me that this is only the beginning.

While Leonardo is at work in the shop, the citizens of Florence witness the completion of the immense building project begun by Filippo Brunelleschi many decades before: finally the dome of the church Santa Maria del Fiore is finished. The last time something so daring was built in Europe was in ancient Roman times, over one thousand years earlier.

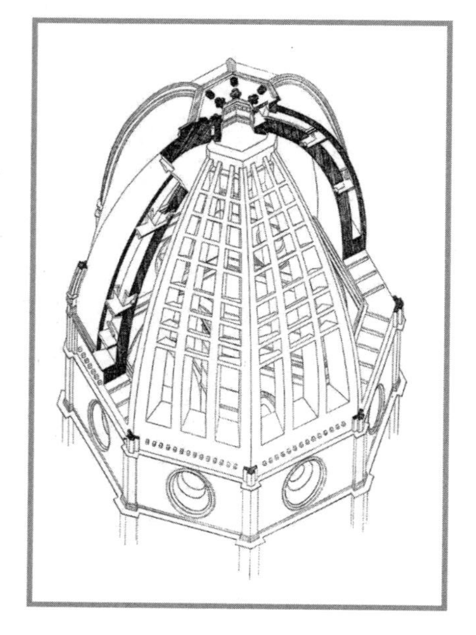

The last of the scaffolding, cranes and machines used to build the dome still have to be taken down. And there's one last detail to be taken care of.

4. You Learn by Doing

I'm right at the very top of the dome. It's a good thing I'm not afraid of heights. I've come to bring a message from Master Verrocchio to the head mason working up here, 80 meters above the ground. The poor guy works, eats, and sleeps here alongside his crew of laborers. Verrocchio was commissioned to forge a huge copper orb to be placed at the crown of the dome, which will reflect the sunlight for hundreds of miles. This glistening orb will be the light of Florence.

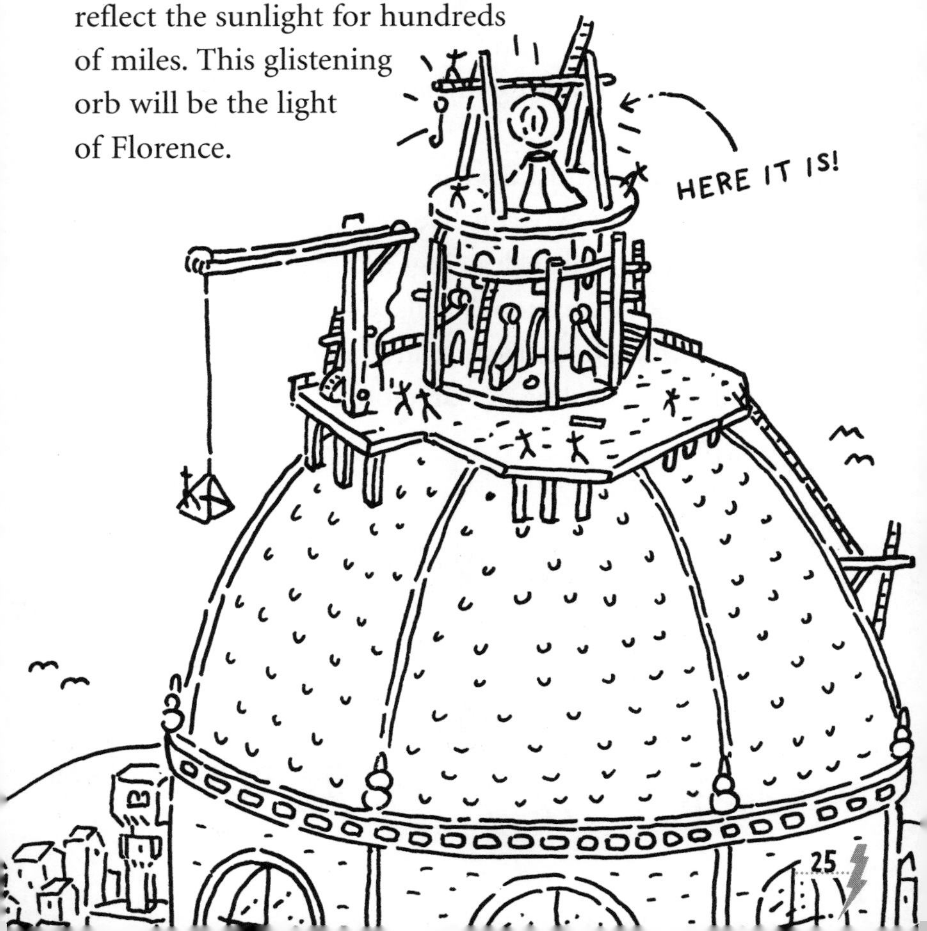

HERE IT IS!

The city looks amazing from up here; the people down on the street look like ants. Because elevators have not been invented yet, in my day you have to climb up and come down the steps, or you can get hoisted up by crane along with the building materials. Speaking of cranes, I've designed one of my own. In the future I'll come up with all sorts of other ideas, you wait and see. In fact, you'll even find plans for a passenger elevator among my notebooks!

Now I'm no longer just drawing. I've learnt to paint expertly. I've been completing my master Verrocchio's drawings and paintings. He reckons I've got exceptional skills. One day he got really mad at me, though, and said that if all his apprentices painted like me, he'd be out of a job!

In a few years I'll be able to enroll in the Guild of St. Luke, the city's association of painters. Then I'll be a professional painter, which is a pretty decent job these days. But I'm also interested in sculpture, and especially in casting bronze statues.

Nowadays, more and more people are demanding this type of commission: suddenly princes all want themselves portrayed on a warhorse, like the emperors of ancient Rome! I'm starting to feel that I want more than the workshop can give me.

This oil painting depicts the "Annunciation". It's the first work that Leonardo did by himself, without the supervision of Master Verrocchio. The scene has a regular layout, and except for a few small liberties, it obeys the rules of perspective.
Each figure and each object in the picture has a precise meaning, and together they tell a story: the angel descends from Heaven, the astonished Virgin raises her hand in alarm. The highly personal style is distinct from earlier models, and even from Leonardo's contemporaries. The work was commissioned from Leonardo by the convent of San Bartolomeo on Monte Oliveto, just outside Florence. By this time, Leonardo's exceptional talent was widely recognized.

5. Artist and Reporter

I'm quite a snappy dresser, and sometimes wear pink tunics that go down to my knees. I also sing and play my own compositions. I've even designed my own lyre, in the shape of a horse's skull. I get invited to private parties at the homes of nobles and all sorts of people in power.

I reckon I can paint just about anything. One day my father brought me a wooden roundel that he wanted me to decorate for one of his agents. So I painted loads of little monsters that looked so scary and realistic that my father first decided to keep it for himself, but then sold it for a fortune!
That's what art's about—astounding people!

On the first day of January 1478 I received my first commission from the city government, in exchange for 25 florins. It was for an altarpiece (a wooden panel) for the Palazzo della Signoria, what you'd call the town hall. But I was never satisfied, and in the end my colleague Filippino Lippi completed it (let's face it, he's less fussy than me!).

This was an unlucky year for Florence. The River Arno burst its banks, and there was flooding everywhere, followed by an epidemic. Worse was still to come, and threatened the very foundations of the community.

On the April 26 two young members of the city's powerful Medici family were ambushed in church. It was organized by the rival Pazzi family. Giuliano Medici was killed, but his brother Lorenzo managed to escape, though badly wounded and bleeding.

A year later, Giuliano Medici's killer was caught and hanged without any trial. I made a sketch of the hanging, like your photojournalist do today. But I was not chosen by the Medici family to do the painting that would immortalize the scene.

Lorenzo and his clan don't like me all that much. They prefer other artists, such as my friend Sandro Botticelli. Frankly, I don't much care for this Lorenzo either. Right now, he is the undisputed lord of Florence. He likes to call himself the "Magnificent", even though he's pretty ugly. And he's pompous, too. He thinks that he's a genius just because he could read Virgil's poems in Latin as a kid. I reckon my future lies far from him and from his ideas about art and life.

This is Lorenzo de' Medici in a portrait by an unknown artist.
Over time, his family of bankers and merchants progressively gained power in Florence, transforming its system of government from that of a free city-state to one ruled by a single prince.

The Medici's bank was so powerful that it lent money to kings and others states. The family owned the finest palaces in town and the biggest farms in the countryside. Like his forebears, Lorenzo saw himself as a man of great culture because he was a patron of painting, sculpture, and poetry. He hosted spectacular celebrations and had wonderful gardens built.
However, his vast libraries contained only volumes written by hand, because he reckoned that books produced on the printing press were tasteless. He did not care about progress in science and technology.
This attitude would eventually harm the city, as well as Leonardo.

6. Better to Emigrate

I'm finding more and more reasons to quit Florence. Along with some other young men, I have even been accused of committing immoral acts. If the accusations go to court, I could be condemned to burn at the stake. In my time judges are very severe about these things.

In the meantime the most talented of my colleagues have been invited by Lorenzo to go to Rome, as a "gift" to Pope Sixtus IV. The pontiff needs frescoes painted in the chapel that will bear his name, the Sistine Chapel. It's a very important job, and I wish I'd been among those chosen for it. But nobody even put forward my name. It's such a bummer.

While there's no shortage of work, I can't seem to stay concentrated on one thing, and tend to squander my energy on a thousand different projects at once. BTW, I've just opened a tavern with my pal Botticelli!

I'm not happy with being just a painter. I feel like there's something missing from the images that I'm creating.

I was commissioned to do a big fresco for the convent of San Donato: the *Adoration of the Magi*. I never finished it, and the monks were real mad at me.

I've started making regular visits to my friend Zoroastro's workshop. He's part craftsman, part artist and part wizard. I bring my designs of the machines that I'd like to build and he makes models of them.

He's the one who will build my flying machine and many other contraptions. But here in Florence I'm seeing less and less of a future for myself, fewer and fewer possibilities.

Milan is the biggest city in northern Italy. In Leonardo's day there were many waterways running through it, powering hundreds of mills. On the man-made canals, called navigli, barges bearing goods and materials make their way through town, right up to the wharf beside the cathedral.

It's a prosperous city: in late medieval Milan, wool was traded, silk was manufactured, and textiles, armor and weapons were produced.

The most imposing building was the vast castle inhabited by the city's prince, Duke Ludovico Sforza. The duke needed artists and painters to beautify his kingdom, but also required engineers and architects for his army and his fortifications.

7. Here I Am in Milan

It took us three days on horseback from Florence to arrive under the city's walls. In your time it would take you just three hours by train or by highway. Duke Ludovico Sforza awaits us, for we come bearing greetings from Lorenzo the Magnificent.

My companion is a young man by the name of Atlante Migliorotti, a lyre player. We've taken lodgings at an inn and will soon be received by the duke.
I have also been invited here as a lyre player: I am to sing some of my new compositions before the duke and his court.

However I'm looking to get hired for an altogether different kind of work. In the letter that I sent to the duke, I describe myself as a talented engineer and inventor of devices and machines for war. I think that these will be the skills that most interest him.

But I have another ace up my sleeve as well. Working at Verrocchio's I learnt the techniques for casting statues. I know what the duke's greatest dream is: he wants a monument in bronze for his father. He wants it to be the grandest equestrian statue ever created. And I know how to do it.

While I'm waiting for my big break to arrive, I've taken on several smaller jobs to fill in time. One of them is a panel painting of the *Virgin of the Rocks*. I'm pretty satisfied with it, but the monks I did it for don't know what to think.

Even some of my fellow artists seem undecided or disapproving. Maybe I am just too modern! On the plus side, I've been invited by the duke to paint a portrait of his beloved companion, the beautiful Cecilia Gallerani, who has taken a liking to me.

It's quite an unusual portrait. She's holding an ermine in her arms. The duke found it so lovely and intense that he will now trust me with anything.

This is the "Lady with an Ermine", the portrait of the lovely Cecilia Gallerani. It's Leonardo's most famous painting after the Mona Lisa. Painted on a small wooden panel (40 cm x 55 cm), the portrait has many hidden and mysterious meanings. Today it is conserved in the National Museum of Kraków, in Poland. Cecilia was only seventeen at the time of the portrait.

The busiest period in Leonardo's career was about to begin.

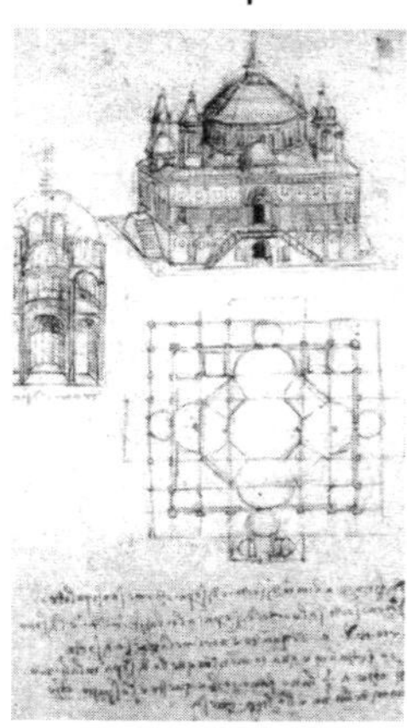

He had finally found a place where his innumerable talents could be put to use and appreciated. At the Sforza court he would meet and befriend Donato Bramante, who was also a painter, but above all a renowned architect. Together, they would devise new solutions for the crossing tower of Milan's enormous cathedral. Meanwhile Leonardo made alterations to the castle, along with palaces, cathedrals and fortifications. His way of thinking had become increasingly scientific as he focused on solutions to concrete problems, even when the city was struck by one of the century's worst calamities.

8. The Plague!

Everything was going well. Duke Ludovico had awarded me a yearly salary of five hundred ducats. That's enough for my clothes, and for room and board in town, just outside the castle.

But then came the plague. The poor began dying in great numbers. The dead were collected from the streets and buried in large common graves. All over the city big bonfires were lit where the clothes and household belongings of those struck with plague were burnt along with sulfur and other smelly substances.

The doctors say that the plague was caused by vapors diffused in the air. But I reckon the disease spread for other reasons: the city is without a proper sewer system, and the filth is everywhere.

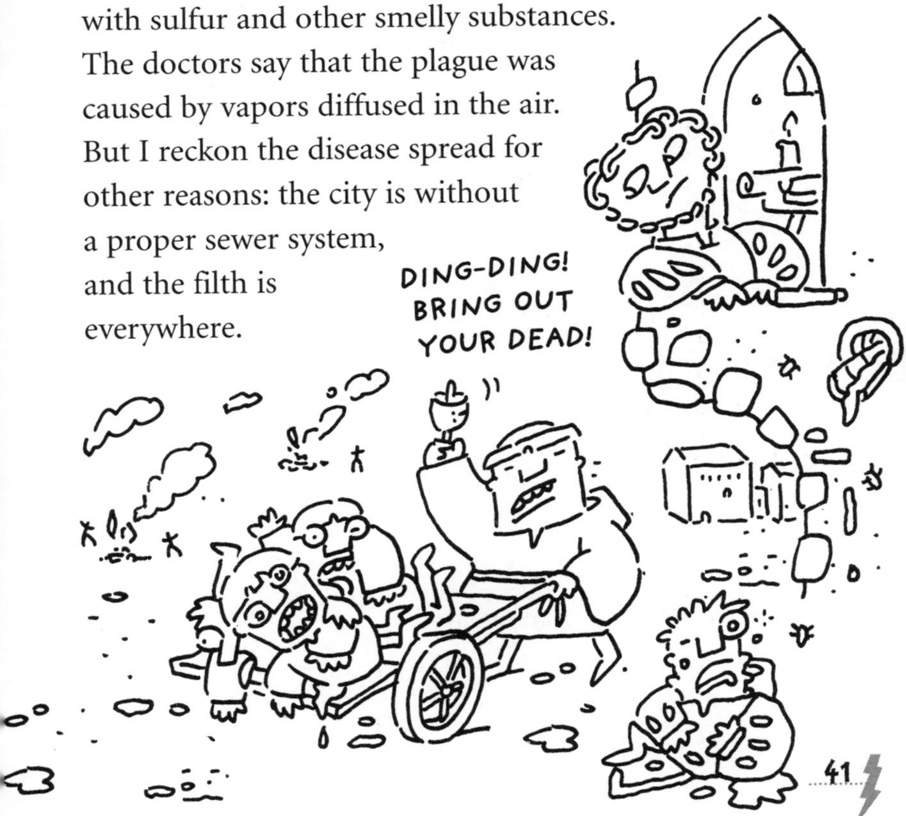

In the countryside it's easier to survive and avoid contagion. That's why the nobles and the rich have fled to their castles and raised the drawbridges to keep people out. But even this may not spare them.

I take my own precautions. I protect my health in a simple and effective way: I wash and keep myself clean. In my day and age, few people bother.

Plus, I haven't eaten the flesh of dead animals for many years now. I am what you guys call a "vegetarian" nowadays.

But to really avoid outbreaks of plague, cities need to be quite different from those of the Medici or Ludovico Sforza. First of all, there would have to be a sewer system to remove all the daily filth and excrement. This system ought to be separate from the system of navigable canals. Houses should be ventilated and dry.

This is my design for the ideal city, which functions on multiple levels. Take a look!

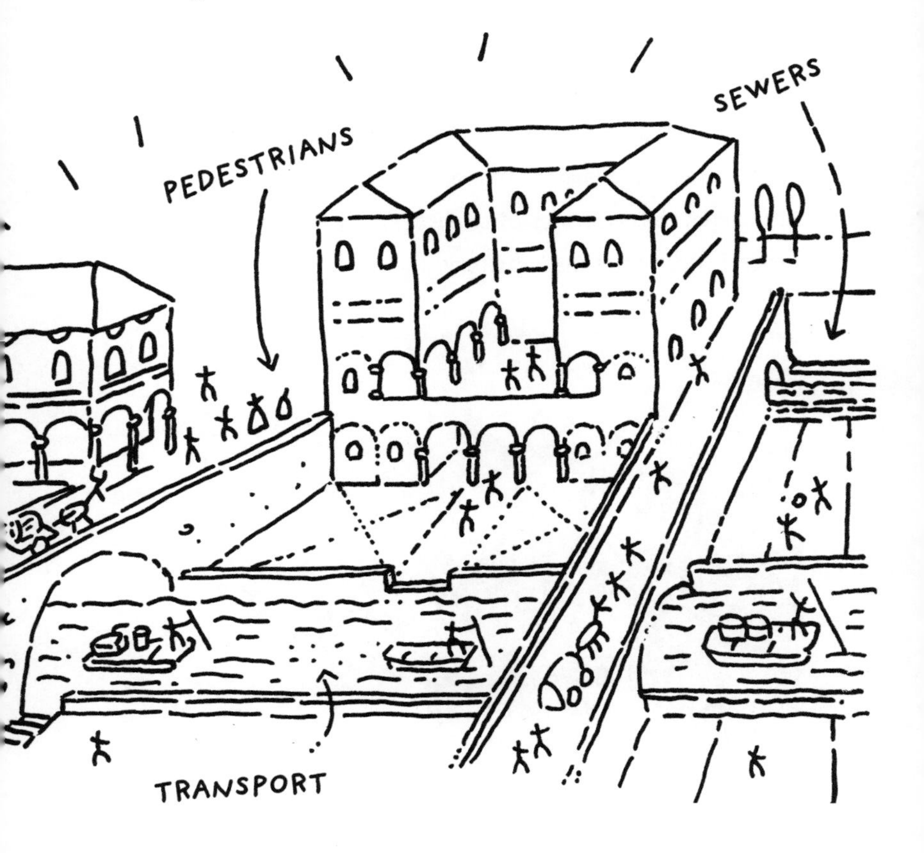

Leonardo was appointed "court engineer" by Duke Ludovico il Moro. As such, he designed new buildings, fortifications, and assorted public utilities. He had to follow work on-site personally. And while he was on the job, he improved the existing tools and machinery, and invented new and more powerful devices such as this "automatic cutter" (right) and an excavator for dredging canals and moats (below)... The duke and his court soon held him in the highest regard, and loved him even more when he put his creativity at the service of celebrations and parties. Several which have made history.

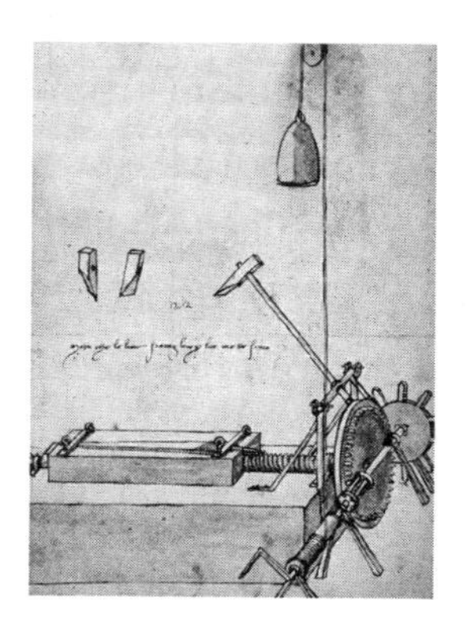

9. The Dance of the Planets

Today is the day of the market in town. I like to mix with the shopkeepers and common folk. I dress like a prince, cut a fine figure, and always have at least one servant with me.

Sometimes I amuse myself by buying caged birds and letting them go free, as they ought to be.

But today I am also here to recruit craftsmen and workers. I am organizing a big festival in honor of Duke Ludovico il Moro. His nephew Gian Galeazzo is marrying the princess Isabella of Aragon. I've been asked to design the costumes, prepare the scenery and direct the entire event, which I can assure you is going to be full of surprises.

The wizardry and many marvels of my mechanical Dance of the Planets will be remembered for a long time. Hundreds of painters and workers were needed to build the complex stage machinery and all the scenery.
I designed most of the costumes myself. An army of expert tailors cut and sewed them together.
One of the big surprises I've prepared is a volcano that erupts with fire and lava. But the most astounding machine I've ever built is one that simulates the movement of the planets. The Stars, Sun, and Moon rotate around the Earth in an amazing dance. I designed it together with the court astrologer. It depicts the glorious horoscope of the two newlyweds.
Unfortunately, the child that played the Sun died afterwards, owing to the gold varnish that was used to paint his body with.

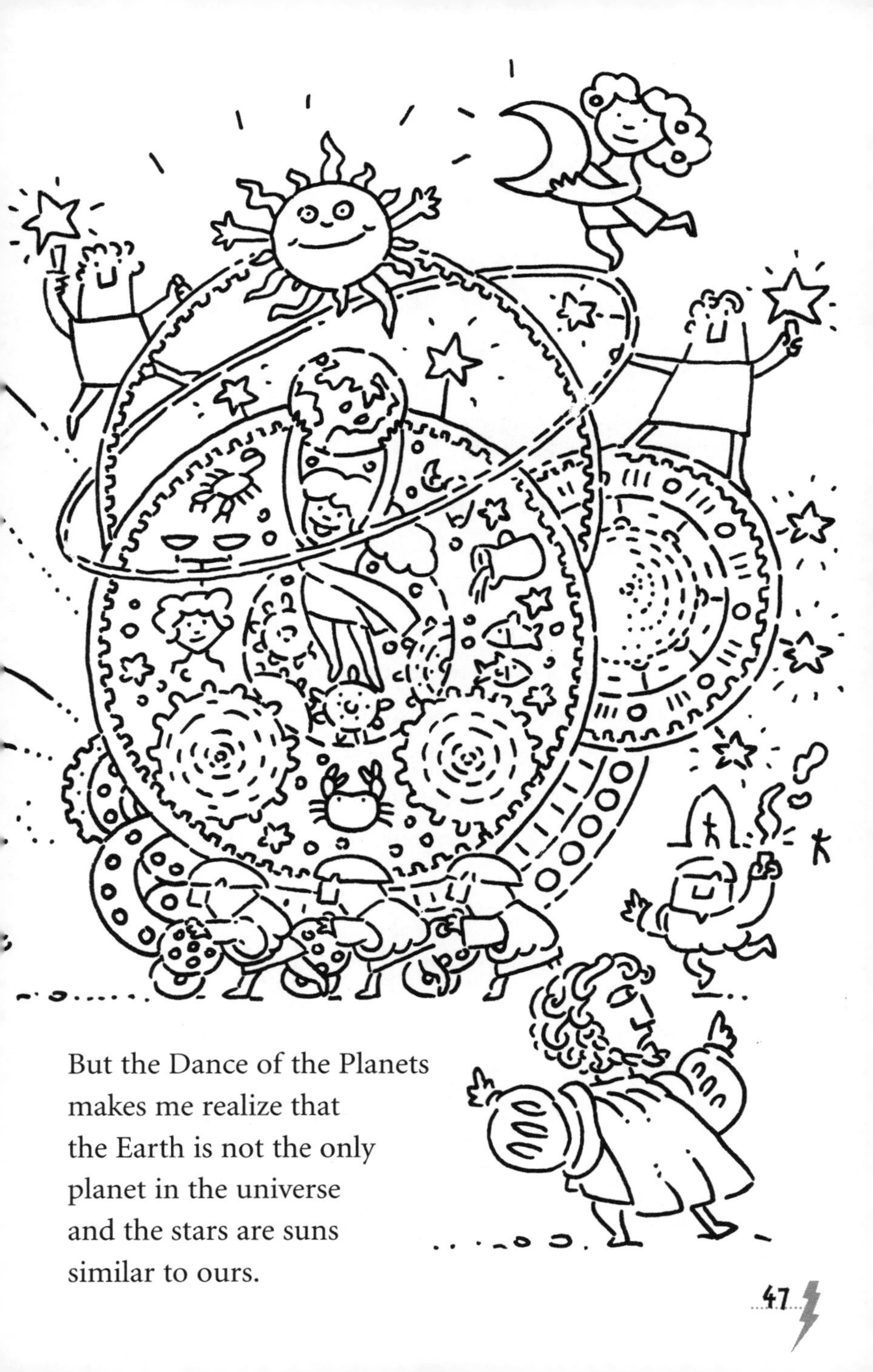

But the Dance of the Planets
makes me realize that
the Earth is not the only
planet in the universe
and the stars are suns
similar to ours.

This is Christopher Columbus. In 1492 this great explorer "discovered" America. His actual reason for sailing across the Atlantic Ocean was to find a new route to India and the Far East, which were becoming increasingly important for Europe because of the trade opportunities they presented. Columbus intended to circumnavigate the globe, which he thought was a lot smaller than it actually is. But along the way he ended up finding an entire new continent. The conquest of the New World would shake up the old equilibrium between peoples and states. But this did not disturb Leonardo's life, for he had grown more intent than ever on inventing new surprises, many of which were designed for a future that was unimaginable at the time.

10. The Pen that Drew the Future

As court engineer, I often have to travel to Duke Ludovico's most distant territories. I often go by horse, alone or with my servants, and always take a notebook and my special pen with me. It's one of a kind, something I designed myself. It has its own reservoir of ink, which allows me to write and draw with the same stroke, and not have to continually dip the nib in an inkwell.

This is the pen I use to write with my special system of moving from right to left. Everything is in reverse, even my signature. At first it might look like some indecipherable code, but it's just specular: all you need to read it is a mirror.
Consider yourself lucky I told you this secret of mine. For centuries, my writings remained a mystery for many people.

And, boy! do I write and draw! I write when needs be and draw when needs be. And believe me, there are some things that remain on the drawing-board, such as my flying machines. Until now, no one had dared to imagine such a device, let alone design one.

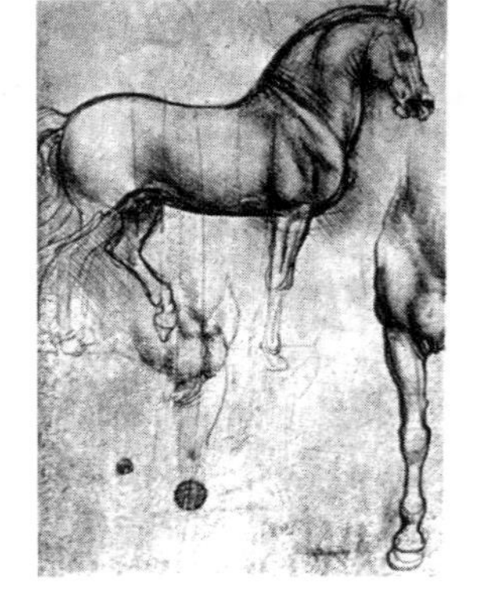

As a painter I am working on a big wall-painting in the refectory of the church of Santa Maria delle Grazie, in Milan. The scene depicted is the *Last Supper*. Even though the painting not finished yet, other painters and folk curious to see the work are coming from all over Europe.

There's been some changes at home too. I've taken on a pageboy named Salaì. As my servant he'll do a bit of everything, even the occasional modeling for some of my paintings. He's irreverent, disrespectful, and a thief to boot… a little devil. But I always forgive him. In some ways he reminds me of myself when I was a child.

There's also a mysterious old lady now living in my house. Don't tell anyone, but it's my mother Caterina. She was widowed, and her only other son was killed in a war. She needed help, and now she's under my care, in my home. It seemed like the right thing to do, although she is a bit disorientated here in Milan.

The monk pictured here is Luca Pacioli. The portrait was painted by Jacopo de' Barbari, a contemporary of Leonardo's. Friar Pacioli lived at court too. He instructed the Duke Ludovico's young heirs in the power of numbers. Leonardo became great friends with Pacioli, and helped him illustrate a book about geometry that the friar was writing. Thanks to Pacioli, Leonardo discovered Euclid and Archimedes. He realized that mathematics and geometry could help him solve concrete problems, for example calculate the amount of bronze needed to construct the enormous horse promised to the duke. But then again, the horse might never get made at all.

11. Clouds of War

Damn and blast! (pardon me…). Everything was going so smoothly here in Milan, with my friends, with work and with my personal studies. I was well loved and much sought after. I had finally completed the clay model for the "great horse" the duke has been waiting so long for. I put the model on display in the middle of courtyard of the Sforza Castle.

The statue was as tall as a three-story building. No one, not even the ancient Greeks or Romans, had ever planned anything so grand. But I hadn't counted on Ludovico's enemies. Over the years they'd become both numerous and powerful.

It would take a huge amount of metal to build the colossal horse: around 80 tons. But now Duke Ludovico needs all the available bronze for a much different purpose.

In the summer of 1499 the armies of Louis XII invaded the Duchy of Milan. The war machines and defense works I had prepared proved useless. In October the French troops entered the city without a single mortar launched or arrow fired. Duke Ludovico abandoned the city, taking his most trusted friends with him. I saw the crowds set his insignia alight in rage. His treasurer, whom I knew well as he was responsible for paying my salary, was captured and bludgeoned to death.

Oppression and abuse by the occupying troops soon followed, to which my model horse fell victim. The crossbowmen that occupied the castle decided to use it for target practice. Amid much laughter and mockery, my clay statue was smashed into a thousand pieces.

I left Milan feeling quite bitter and disappointed. My life was at a turning point.

At 48 years of age Leonardo found himself suddenly unemployed, but by this point his name was on the lips of half of Europe's princes and rulers. Stories and legends preceded him wherever he went. He would be well received anywhere. But there was a growing problem: he did not know how to keep his papers safe and organize his innumerable discoveries and inventions. By this time he had thousands of papers and sketches, only a small part of which would then be collected and published in what would later be known as his "notebooks" or "codices."

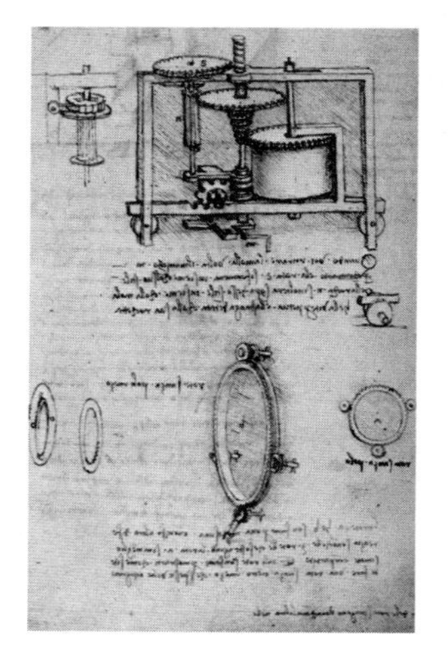

Leonardo thought of compiling a dictionary of at least 3,000 illustrated terms: including a table lamp with adjustable intensity, automatic doors, siphon drains for emptying canals, contact lenses for older folks, a parachute, a tank, helicopter and automobile...

12. The Wandering Scientist

Here I'm in a place called Vaprio d'Adda, a little riverside town to the north of Milan. I like places like this, so full of water and greenery. I have some good friends here, and my papers are safe.

My protector Ludovico il Moro is in exile, and Milan is still under French occupation. Given the circumstances, I've decided to accept an invitation from Isabella d'Este to be her guest in the splendid city of Mantua. The Marquise Isabella has offered me a job as a military adviser. But what she really wants is something else altogether: to have me paint her portrait. So I've begun to draw her in profile.

The lady is rather disagreeable and unpleasant, however. She insists on choosing the colors herself, along with the composition and subject. I just can't stand her.

In the end I quit, so the Marquise Isabella never got her portrait.

I am now the honored guest of the Most Serene Republic of Venice, the most liberal and enlightened state of the entire era. But I have arrived at what is perhaps the most critical time in its thousand-year history. For the realm is about to be attacked by the Ottoman Turks, whose forces have begun to invade its outlying territories. The threat is serious and frankly terrifying. I've been appointed military adviser, and as such I propose to divert a river to engulf the enemy.

My plan of attack involves
the use of scuba divers
and underwater saboteurs!
But all my advice is being
ignored. I've run up
against hoary admirals
with outdated ideas.
And as I don't like being
ignored, I'm leaving.
Pity really, because
I really like Venice.

Leonardo decided to return to Florence for a while. He found the place greatly changed. Lorenzo the Magnificent had died meanwhile, and the Medici family no controled the city. Among the newer generation was a promising young man named Niccolò Machiavelli (left). He and Leonardo become friends. Machiavelli had been developing a study of human behavior and had begun to apply his observations to politics, to rulers and the ruled. But these were dark times: in the streets of Florence one could still smell the stench of the stake upon which the Dominican friar Gerolamo Savonarola was burnt. He had preached against corruption, but had gone too far. Previously, he had he ensured that many paintings he considered immoral were destroyed by fire, even some of Botticelli's. In the end, the friar too would perish in the flames. Given the situation, Leonardo thought it best to accept a job that would have him once again roaming around Italy.

13. In the Service of a Killer

Here I am with Cesare Borgia. My friend Machiavelli says that Borgia is the best prince of the day. This is because he's the only one who has the talents and willpower to bring together all the little states that Italy is divided into.

Cesare Borgia has hired me as a military engineer. He pays very well, and treats me with respect. That's because he needs me. The fortifications of his cities are all in desperate need of repair. Today armies come wielding mortars and cannons. The old type of city walls can't withstand the kind of missiles launched with these new weapons. So the defense works all need what you people nowadays call a "makeover.

The problem with Cesare Borgia is his murderous temperament. He doesn't look anybody in the eye, not even friends or family members. If someone is in the way of his plans, he simply kills them without much hesitation. He's not too picky about how: by poison, the sword, strangling… as long as it's done quickly. Good thing that all I have to do for him is design fortifications and new defense works.

Another thing I do for Cesare Borgia is draw maps of his cities, for military and defensive purposes, such as this one of Imola. The innovative thing about these maps is that they are drawn to scale, and are oriented according to the four points of the compass. Most importantly of all, they're extremely precise. This is quite novel in my day.

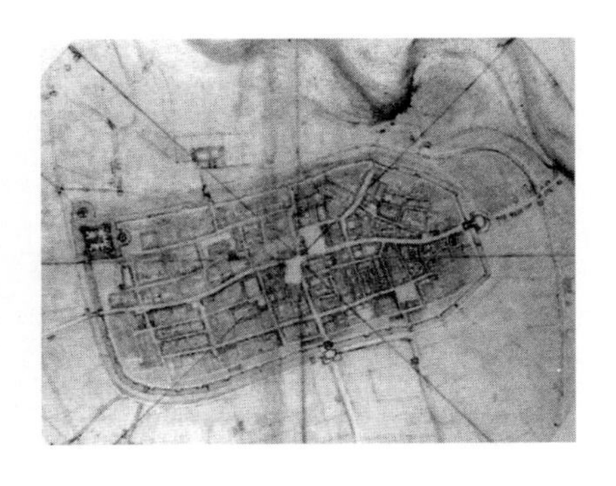

But Cesare Borgia grew increasingly insufferable and terrible. Even some of his most faithful supporters—a group that includes some close friends of mine—finally had enough and rebelled. They just wanted him to behave more… like a human being.
In response Cesare invited them to his palace. They accepted, and came and sat at his table, at which point he had them all strangled. I think it's time to move on. Before it's too late…

His experiences with Cesare Borgia made Leonardo's name as a military expert, and from then on he was much sought after and feared by princes and governments. He was considered unsurpassed as a planner of fortifications. But he had also designed and improved upon many war machines, such as this catapult and the "machine-gun" mortar pictured below.

By this time, his physical appearance had begun to resemble that of the wise old man we are all familiar with: a flowing beard and long white hair.

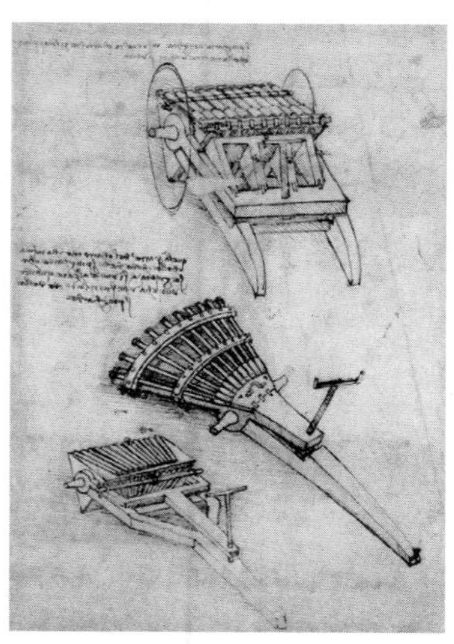

When he returned Florence as a military consultant to the Republic, he believed that by now he had no rivals. But instead he found a quite formidable one, in the field that troubled him most—the arts.

14. An Unbearable Antagonist

Here I am back in Florence. I've was welcomed with great honors. They show utmost respect and pay me handsomely. But it didn't take long before things went sour. I'm really upset about a young sculptor named Michelangelo Buonarroti. Everybody's constantly heaping praise upon him—too much praise, to my mind. Everywhere I go, there he is: on the street, in the squares and at the parties given by the nobles. He claims that sculpture is superior to painting. How dare he! He's even told me that painting is for ladies, and for people with delicate hands like mine. So I grabbed an iron bar and bent it before his eyes. "Straighten that if you can, big strong sculptor man!" They say that he replied with one of his rhymes, but I didn't catch it.

But let's get back to concrete things. I'm here as a military expert, and our formidable and long-time foe, the Republic of Pisa, has once again declared war on us. Pisa is situated along the River Arno, like Florence, but it's much closer to the sea. I've proposed a plan to divert the Arno and leave Pisa and its people high and dry. The river would flow south and flood other enemy territories. Even Machiavelli supports my plan. But it would take thousands of men to do the job. This has led me to devise and draw up the plans for huge excavators, machines on a scale never before imagined. The idea was first conceived for military ends, but I'm also thinking about how to use the power of the water that will be unleashed: I'm picturing

HE CAN
EVEN CREATE
AN ARTIFICIAL
VALLEY!

the Arno valley populated with factories, mills of all sorts, ironworks…

The excavation work had just begun when the government changed its mind. No, the Arno was not to be diverted. But meanwhile they gave me another grandiose task: painting a big wall in the largest room of the government's palace. It was to be a war scene: the Battle of Anghiari, where the Florentines defeated Milan in 1440.

I'm pleased to have the job. There's just one problem. On the opposite wall, that insolent fop Michelangelo Buonarroti has been asked to paint an equally grand fresco, depicting the battle of Cascina.
I could strangle him!

Leonardo put all of his experience and knowledge into the great mural in Government Hall in Florence. He also experimented with new paints and a new procedure for drying them with the heat from giant braziers. But the heat ended up melting the paints and ruining the work he had done. Furious, Leonardo left the job unfinished. He would never resume work on it again.

For his part, Michelangelo had only managed to do some drawings on paper before he was summoned to Rome, where he would paint his famous frescoes (The Last Judgment) in the Sistine Chapel. Thus the contest between the two greatest artists and architects of the Renaissance ended without ever even having really begun. There would never be another chance to compare their work side-by-side in the same place. In the meantime, Leonardo had also begun his most famous portrait: his sitter this time was Mona Lisa, wife of the Florentine banker Francesco del Giocondo. But he would never deliver it to its patron. Instead, he would take it with him wherever he went, retouching and perfecting it for the rest of his life.

15. On the Move Again

This is Charles d'Amboise, Marshal of France and current Governor of Milan. He invited me to join his court. I'm so glad to get away from Florence. Meanwhile, news came that my father died, leaving ten sons and two daughters, plus myself. This flock of half-siblings want the inheritance all for themselves. They even intend to claim the farm that Uncle Francesco left to me. I can't stand this sort of thing.

But back in Milan I found many friends both old and new. And a lot of nice jobs: designing a garden with aviaries, fountains and waterworks. I organize parties featuring elaborate works of art composed of—guess what—fruit and vegetables!

I'm trying to put my writings in order. Many of my papers are here in Milan. Along with Salaì, now I also I have a young man named Francesco Melzi helping me, the scion of a noble family of Vaprio d'Adda.

At present I'm studying light and vision. I've come to think that light travels in waves. I'm carrying out experiments in optics with glass lenses. I've come close to the idea of the telescope, and I've even built something very similar to a projector.

My studies in anatomy are also moving forward. I had first begun them to help with my art, but I later discovered that they are also useful for solving mechanical and architectural problems. The human body is a perfect machine, with a perfect architecture.

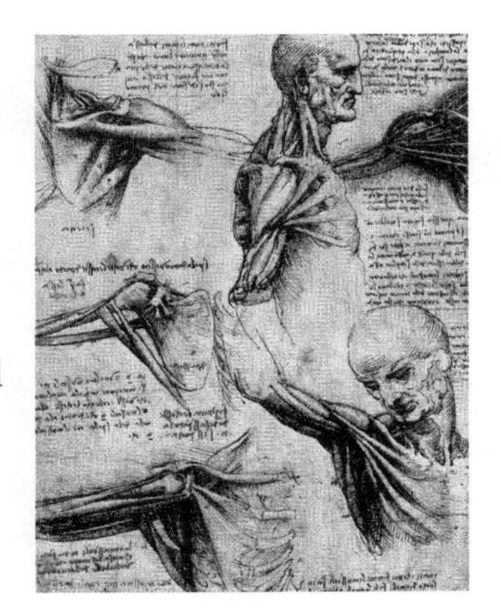

Unfortunately, clouds of war are once again gathering over the Italian peninsula. The French will soon be driven out of Milan. And so I must pack my bags once more. For now, I'm heading to Vaprio d'Adda, after that I've no idea where I'll go.

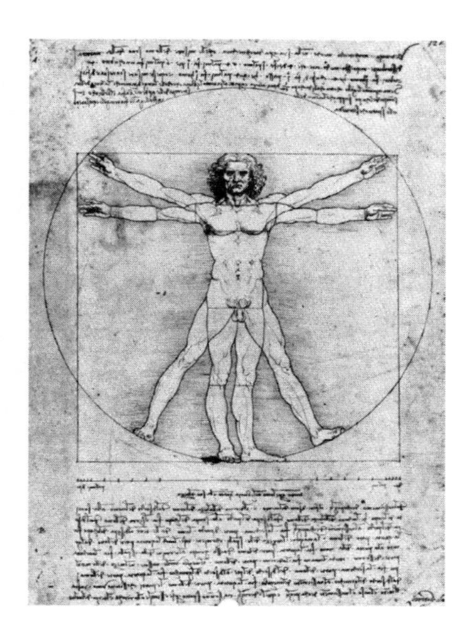

This drawing of Leonardo's is known as the "Vitruvian Man" because it illustrates a chapter of a book by the famous ancient Roman engineer and architect Vitruvius, which describes the proportions of the human body.

Leonardo was fascinated by ancient Rome and would soon have the chance to see it in person. For he did not stay long in his country getaway. He soon received an invitation from the new pope, who took the name Leo X. He arrived in Rome in the autumn of 1513, with his servants and belongings: clothes, his lute, a chest full of drawings and notes and, of course, the Mona Lisa. But the atmosphere he found there did not prove very favorable to his research and work.

16. Rome

I had never seen it before.
The ruins are really impressive!
These ancient Romans
were truly amazing
engineers and architects.

It is today's Rome that's the problem, where I don't feel at ease. Pope Leo X claims to love science and the arts, but he's got his own personal idea of what painting is. So he gives the most interesting jobs to younger lads like Raphael and Michelangelo.

NOT THAT BLASTED MICHELANGELO AGAIN!

I have time to further my studies of anatomy. But I'm being spied on by the two assistants that were assigned to me. When they saw me dissect a cadaver, they got scared and publicly accused me of witchcraft. As a result the pope himself has banned any further research. Everyone's talking about it now…

So the Romans want a sorcerer do they? Then that's what they'll get! I decided to have a bit of fun, and prepared a practical joke for anyone who came to nosey around the house. I invited one of these intruders into a room where I'd installed a cow's intestine that can be inflated to fill the entire room. The poor chap hadn't a clue what was happening, and thought the room was getting smaller and screamed in terror!

For fun, I trained a big lizard and taught him to jump up on my shoulders. I glued two frightening horns to his head, plastered a dozen fake eyes on his body, and fitted two wings that moved as he walked. The result was a charming little dragon! I carried him around in a crate, and brought him with me to the halls of the Vatican. Then I released him and sat back to enjoy the ensuing terror.

I also built little dragons out of colored paper and launched them from my windows. They were just tiny gliders, but I can assure you that in the eyes of this city's superstitious citizens, they looked like little infernal monsters and were far more terrifying than any UFO of your time.

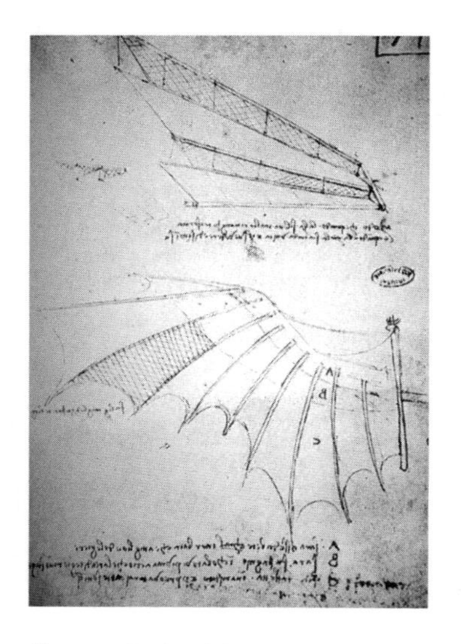

The little flying monsters that Leonardo flung from his windows were only harmless toys. But actually, for a long time he had been at work on a manned flying machine. He studied closely how birds fly, designed artificial wings, and built mechanisms for moving them.

Some of his flying machines, if powered by motors or made with modern synthetic materials, would work quite well today. But in the 16th century, attempting human flight in one of his contraptions was a dangerous undertaking. Many had a go at it all the same, including Zoroastro, Leonardo's wizard-craftsman friend.

17. Promoted to Ambassador

I don't know about you, but I hate mosquitoes.
And there are swarms of them in Pontine Marshes, a vast unhealthy area to the south of Rome. The pope has charged me with devising a scheme for draining all these bogs. It's no small task. To begin with I have to draft a map of the area, and then trace onto it the canals that will divert the stagnant water into the sea.
It will probably be the greatest hydraulic project carried out in this century. These lands will soon be inhabited and cultivated, thanks to me!

I am always looking at the world around me. I watch the waves of the sea as they break on the shore in the distance. I think about the way water influences a landscape. I believe that everything in this world is gradually changing under the effect of atmospheric agents, or of man. I'd like to collect all my thoughts and drawings about water together in one book.

Meanwhile in Rome young Raphael has been promoted to head architect of the new St. Peter's. The pope forgot me yet again… Instead he has made me an ambassador, and is sending me to meet with the new French king, Francis I, whose great army has invaded Italy again.

I speak French well and was welcomed by his court. I reached him in Bologna, where I organized celebrations in his honor. As a gift to symbolize peace, I built him a robot shaped like a golden lion. I designed it to walk up to the king, and then open up and drop hundreds of white lilies at his feet, the symbol of the French crown.

I like this young man…
When he is at the head of his troops, he wears gold-plated armor. He stands six feet tall, which is pretty tall for a man of my day: a good 8 inches above the average height. But most importantly, he admires me as a scientist and is very curious about all my experiments.

Meet Francis I, King of France, in a portrait done during the years of his descent into Italy. King Francis once again subjugated the Duchy of Milan and made alliances with all of the other sovereigns of the peninsula. At this time he was the most powerful man in Europe. He was passionate about science and the arts, and invited Leonardo to come back to France with him, offering him a huge salary, a princely residence, and all the time and resources he needed to continue his research and continue painting. Leonardo accepted.

To reach the king, he had to undertake an exhausting journey on horseback all the way from Rome to Amboise in France. Nowadays to travel the same distance would only take a dozen hours or so by car.

18. Twilight Years of Peace in France

Here I am in the castle of King Francis.

I'm living in a comfortable country house, surrounded by a garden and an orchard bordering the castle. The castle towers above the town of Amboise and the River Loire. Amboise lies about 100 miles southwest of Paris. It took me three months to reach it from Rome, loaded down with all my baggage, paintings, and notes… I traveled with Salaì, Melzi and a small group of servants and assistants. King Francis has awarded me a salary of 1,000 gold scudi. That's an astronomical sum, comparable to the signing fee of certain football players in your time.

King Francis is young but he's a good listener, and likes learning from me. But I'm also learning plenty from him, too. He often comes to visit me and ask for advice. There's an underground passage linking my house to the castle. As with the others, for him too I design castles, land reclamation schemes, and stage scenery, but unlike them he doesn't think of me as merely a servant, however brilliant and capable… for him I am a friend, something of a wizardly confidant.

But the years have taken their toll. I am an old man now, full of aches and pains. I have arthritis in my hands, making it hard to write and draw. Melzi and Salaì help me to complete my last paintings, such as the one of *St. John the Baptist* pointing towards heaven.

And so on 23 April 1519 I made my will. I am leaving my half-siblings everything that I left behind in Italy, including an account of 400 scudi, and the small property inherited from Uncle Francesco.

TO SALAÌ I LEAVE A VINEYARD AND 100 GOLDEN SCUDI...

TO FRANCESCO MELZI ALL OF MY DRAWINGS...

I'm bequeathing something for all my servants and collaborators. And to young Melzi I have bequeathed my most precious legacy.

Leonardo left his world on 2 May 1519. He went in peace, surrounded by the affection of his friends. A legend tells how the king of France ran to his bedside for a last goodbye. He's buried in Amboise, in a chapel near the castle.
Leonardo's name soon became legend: in the arts, in science, in technology. There's no field in which he did not leave some trace or invention. Everything he did is documented in the priceless legacy of writings and sketches that he entrusted to his friend Francesco Melzi.
Unfortunately when Melzi returned to Italy, he only managed to put together the Treatise on Painting. *After his death the remaining material was left forgotten in the attic of the Melzi house in Vaprio d'Adda, then later dispersed and some parts lost. Only much later (decades, even centuries afterwards) the more than 3,500 pages written and drawn by Leonardo were gradually put in order and bound in "codices", known as the Codex Madrid, the Codex Foster, and the Codex Windsor...*

The most largest of these bound volumes is given the name Codex Atlanticus *because of its Atlas-like size, or perhaps in reference to the mythical Atlas, who according to the ancient Greeks bore the Earth on his shoulders, and indeed Leonardo's notebook carries a truly enormous quantity of knowledge.*

The rediscovery and cataloguing of Leonardo's notebooks is not yet finished, and there are still surprises in store. One thing is certain however: if Leonardo's work had been correctly interpreted, organized and made known from the beginning, civilization would have advanced to its current state centuries earlier. Perhaps Napoleon would have traveled by airplane and we would have already colonized all of the planets in the Solar System.

. C VIII .
DVODECEDRON ABSCI
SVS ELEVATVS VACVVS .

A Leonardian Dictionary

ABACUS

Counting tool consisting of a frame with beads. It was invented in the Orient and introduced in Europe at the end of the Middle Ages. At “abacus school” Leonardo learned how to use it to perform quite complicated mathematic operations.

ALCHEMY

The art that aimed to transform common metals into gold, in part through the quest for the mythical Philosopher’s Stone. But it also contained the sum of the knowledge of chemistry and metallurgy in Leonardo’s day. In this sense, Leonardo was an alchemist.

ANATOMY

The study of the body and organs of a living being. Leonardo dissected corpses so as to make detailed drawings of their insides. For doing this, he was accused of sorcery.

ARCHIMEDES

Engineer and philosopher from the city of Syracuse in Sicily, born around 297 BCE. His machinery was studied by the Arabs, and then rediscovered by the Europeans toward the end of the Middle Ages. Leonardo was a great admirer of his work, and even tried to build one of the man's fabled mirrors, with which he reportedly destroyed the enemy warships.

ARCHITECTURE

The art and technique of designing buildings and other large-scale works. Leonardo designed castles, cathedrals, and once even an entire city.

ART

As for the ancient Greeks and Romans, for Leonardo "art" meant knowing how to do something well. In this way, everything he turned his hand to, was done with skill and know-how. And of course immense talent.

AUTOMATON

A moving mechanical device that imitates a human being or animal. During his career, Leonardo built several huge mechanical devices for entertainment. They were powered by complex series of springs and counterweights that drove cogs and pulley mechanisms.

AUTOMOBILE

By definition an "auto-mobile" is a vehicle on wheels powered by an internal motor. Leonardo designed one that moved autonomously thanks to a system of springs.

AUTOMATIC ROASTING SPIT

The roasting spit was a very common item in Leonardo's day. He invented one that rotated automatically, powered by the hot air that rose up the chimney.

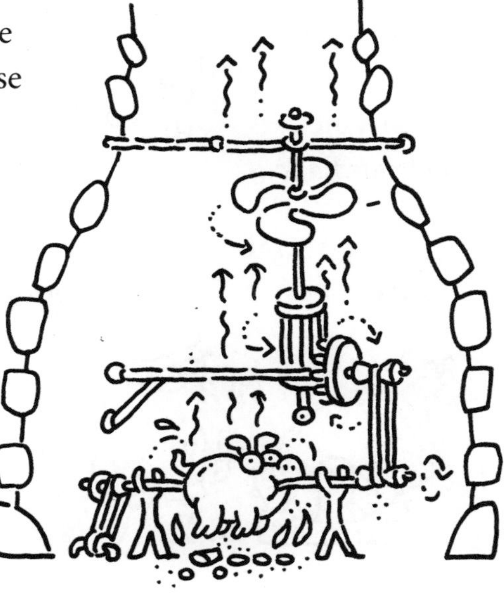

BEATING WINGS

The organ that allows birds to fly. Leonardo studied the flight of birds, and designed various kinds of wings and machines that simulated their movement.

BICYCLE

Leonardo's plans for a modern bicycle were rediscovered during the restoration the *Codex Atlanticus*. The drawing, despite many doubts, has been attributed to Salaì, Leonardo's sly and mischievous servant. You can see an amazing three-dimension recreation of Leonardo's bicycle at the Museo Leonardiano in Vinci. *www.museoleonardiano.it*

BOMBARD

A primitive kind of cannon, which shot big stone or iron balls.

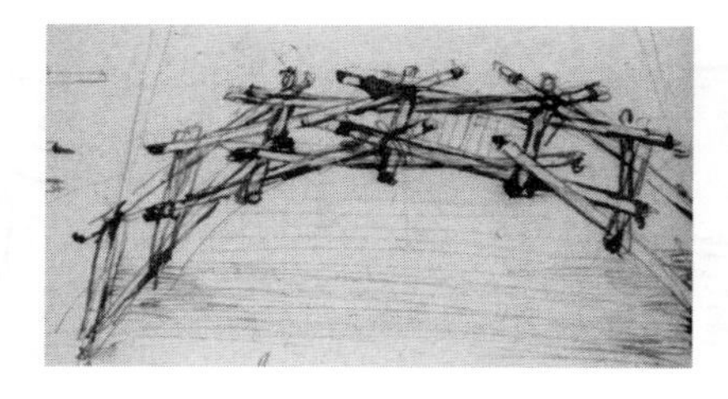

BRIDGES

Leonardo designed many of them, even an enormous one for the strait of Dardanelles, commissioned by the Caliph of Constantinople. But Leonardo's most interesting bridges are the mobile ones that are designed to be assembled quickly, like this one, requiring simple wooden stakes. If you fancy a challenge, try building a small version of one of Leonardo's bridges out of matchsticks!

BULLETS

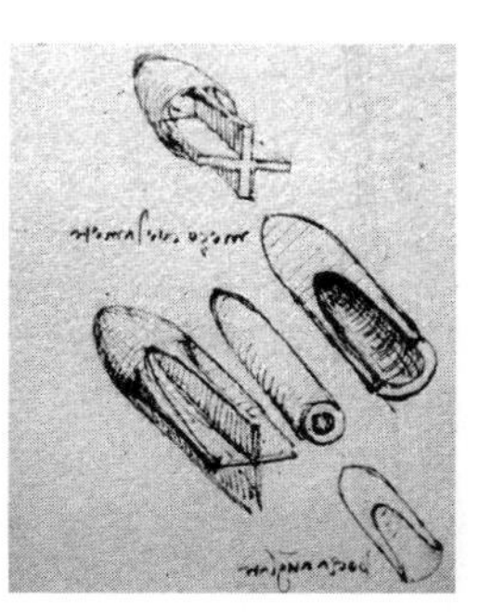

Leonardo studied the effects of air on the trajectory of projectiles. His research led to his designs of a series of bullets with a more aerodynamic form resembling those used in modern weapons.

CANAL

A manmade waterway for irrigation or navigation. In his lifetime, Leonardo planned and oversaw the creation of many navigable canals.

CANAL POUNDS

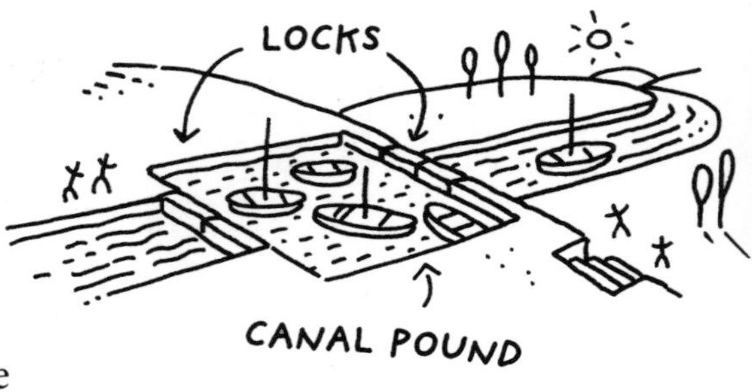

An enclosure of water of varying sizes contained between two locks on a canal, to enable barges and boats to proceed upstream.

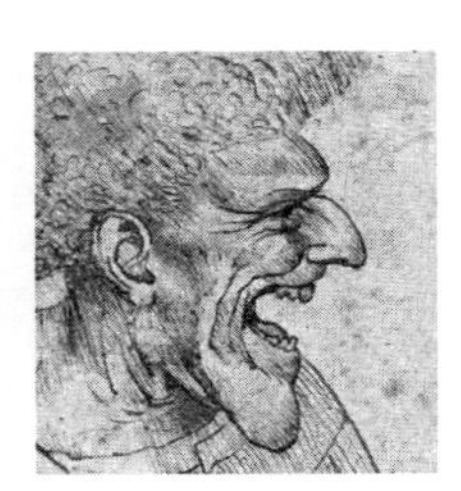

CARICATURE

A portrait that exaggerates the physical and psychological characteristics of its subject. Leonardo drew many of them of people of his time.

CASTING

The art and technique of creating statues, cannons, and other objects in bronze. The stages involved:

1. first making a clay model of the desired object ;
2. then creating an identical version in wax;
3. then forming a clay mold around the wax model;

CARTOONS

Before painting a large fresco painters would make a series of drawings on paper in preparation. These works were called "cartoons". Of some of Leonardo's works only the cartoons have survived, which today are worth millions of euro.

4. pouring molten bronze into the mold;
5. letting it cool;
6. breaking open the mold.

CLAY

Grayish earth that can be shaped into anything, and then baked in an kiln, or oven. Vases, small statues, and models for bronze casting were all made with clay.

CONTACT LENSES

Leonardo discovered the principle of artificial lenses (envisaging their possible use for improving the eyesight of older people) during his anatomy studies on the eyeballs, which he used to preserve boiled in egg-whites!

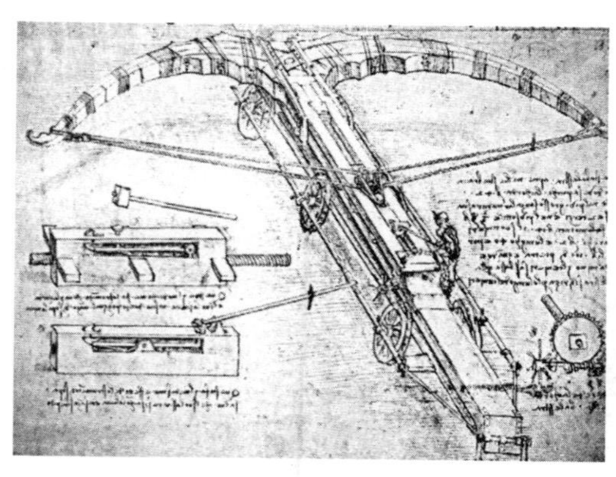

CROSSBOW

A weapon consisting of a shaft fitted with a bow that was pulled taut and released via a trigger-like device, firing a bolt or similar projectile. Leonardo designed some enormous ones withmultiple shafts that could fire in quick succession.

DESIGNER

Architect or engineer that projects (and draws) beautiful and useful objects.

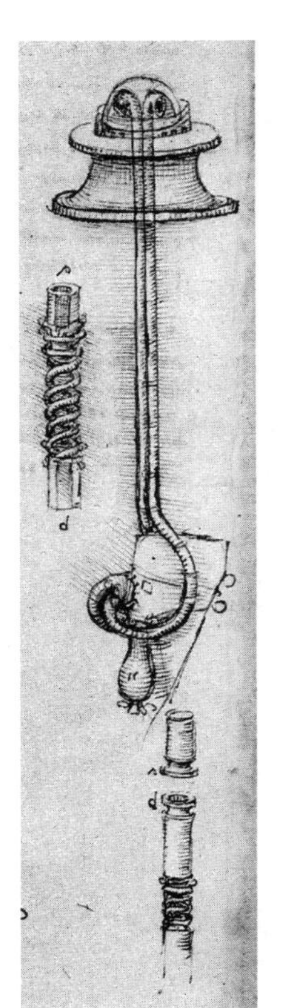

DIVING SUIT

Leonardo designed it for walking under water, in order to sneak up on enemy ships and sabotage them!

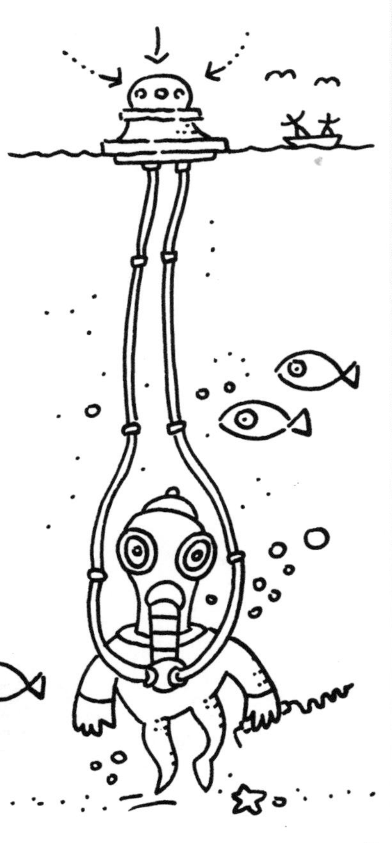

DRAGONS

Mythical creatures that were very popular in the Middle Ages. Leonardo built various mechanical dragons as practical jokes and frightened the wits out of many an unsuspecting passer-by!

EXTRA-TERRESTRIALS

Some of Leonardo's inventions seem so modern for his time that some writers have thought that they must have an extra-terrestrial origin.

FLIPPERS

Leonardo designed them for use on the hands, anticipating the ones used today for the feet.

FORTIFICATIONS

Around the year 1500 in Europe various types of firearm (mortars and cannons) entered widespread use, and gradually replaced mechanical weapons such as crossbows and catapults. The early defensive walls and crenelated towers proved inadequate against the new weaponry, and so Leonardo equipped them with cannon platforms and stronger, rounded towers.

FRESCO

A painting done on plaster while it is still wet. Leonardo made use of alchemy to produce the pigments he would then use in his paintings.

GREAT FLOOD

In Leonardo's day it was widely believed that the Great Flood, as told by the Bible, had submerged the entire Earth and given it its present appearance.

HELICOPTER

Leonardo designed an "air-screw" or rotor that would provide a form of lift-off similar to that of the modern helicopter.

HORSE

Leonardo studied the anatomy of the most beautiful horses of his day in order to create the famous equestrian statue for Duke Ludovico il Moro. Five centuries later two reproductions of Leonardo's gigantic bronze horse were created by an American named Charles Dent and the sculptor Nina Akamu, who closely followed Leonardo's sketches. One was installed in Milan's hippodrome in September 1999, and another in Grand Rapids, Michigan, the following October.
www.leonardoshorse.org

KITE

Bird of prey of a size and appearance halfway between an eagle and a falcon, which was common in central and southern Europe.

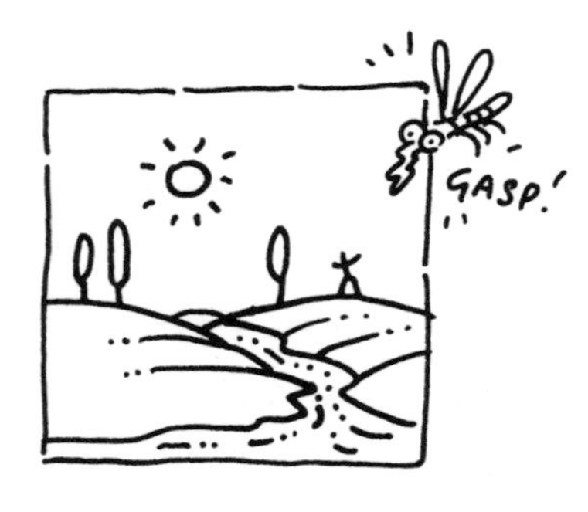

RECLAMATION

The process of building canals to get rid of the stagnant water from unhealthy swamplands, so that the land can then be cultivated. Mosquitoes hate reclamation projects.

LEFT-HANDEDNESS

The tendency to use the left hand instead of the right. By no means a defect—many great figures of the past were left-handed, and Leonardo was the greatest of them all.

LEONARDO'S CODICES

A codex (pl. codices) was a book written and illustrated by hand. It was not until after his death that Leonardo's notes and drawings were collected into the famous codices we know today, each on having a distinct name, such as the *Codex Trivulzianus* (in Milan), the *Codex Windsor* (in Windsor Castle, England), the *Codex Hammer* containing Leonardo's observations on hydraulics and water, the *Codex on the flight of Birds*, with all of his studies of flight and designs for airborne devices.

LIFEBUOY

Leonardo designed a circular lifesaver that's very similar to those used today.

C'MON EVERYONE— JUMP IN!

MAPS

It was only in Leonardo's time that maps of cities and regions began to be made "to scale", that is in proportion to actual distances. But people were still very far from having a realistic perception of the true size of the world.

MILL

A machine for grinding grain or other materials. Water-powered mills worked by means of a wheel driven by water. This wheel could also move other gears that in turn would move trip-hammers, bellows, presses, and other simple machines in use in Leonardo's day.

MILLSTONE

Even though he was the military consultant of princes and states, Leonardo also invented and improved upon a great number of machines with a peaceful use, utilized in the countryside and in cities. Like this one, which could grind corn while separating the flour from the bran.

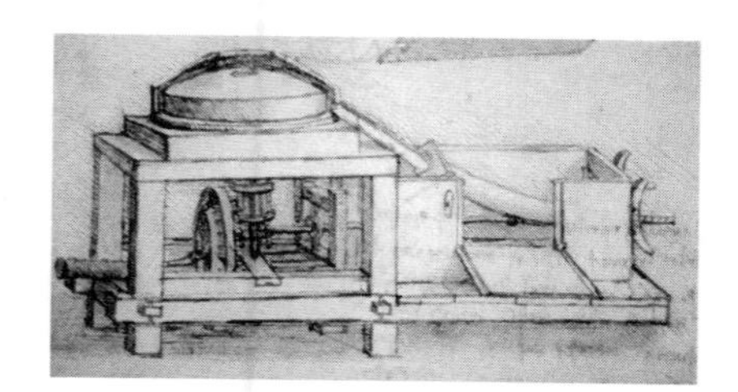

PAINTING

In Leonardo's time, artists painted on wooden panels. For his famous paintings Leonardo experimented with new pigments and techniques that were not always as successful as he hoped.

IT WORKED EVEN BACK IN THE 1500s!

PARACHUTE

The one Leonardo invented is shaped like a pyramid.

PEN

Leonardo designed a writing instrument that is very similar to the modern fountain-pen, by perfecting a model used by the ancient Egyptians.

PRINTING PRESS

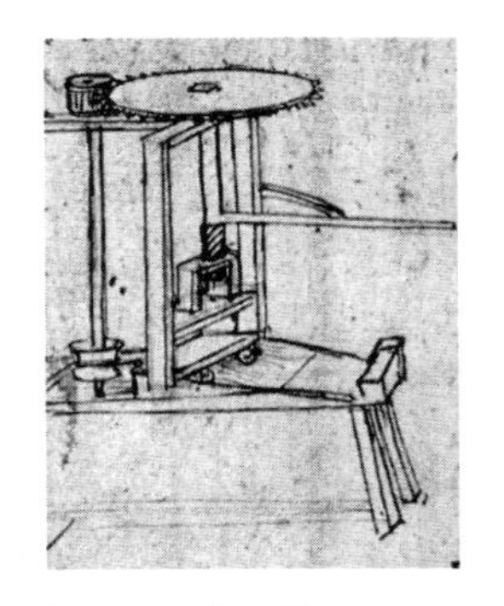

Leonardo introduced some innovations to this machine, which was already in use throughout Europe in his day. However, none of his own works would ever be printed in his lifetime. It was not until more than a century after his death that the first, the *Treatise on Painting*, would appear in print.

SELF-PORTRAIT

We know how Leonardo looked as an old man, thanks to this famous self-portrait. The original drawing is kept in the Royal Library of Turin.

SPECIAL EFFECTS

Leonardo invented many, using his knowledge of alchemy. During a celebration at the Sforza Castle he made a miniature volcano that spewed forth smoke and lava.

STYLIST

Designer of fashion and exclusive outfits. Leonardo designed clothes, hats and extraordinary costumes for celebrations and ceremonies.

SUBMERSIBLE

Leonardo designed several types of submarine, which he proposed for use in the war between the Venetians and the Turks.

SYSTEM FOR WALKING ON WATER

Curious equipment designed by Leonardo, consisting of floating shoes and walking poles to maintain one's balance on water surfaces.

TANK

Invented by Leonardo. Shaped like a flying saucer, the vehicle was powered by soldiers inside its shell.

TREATISE ON PAINTING

Collection of all Leonardo's writings and sketches on the topic, treated as a science. This was the first collection of texts and drawings by Leonardo to be printed in book form. The first edition dates from 1651.

URBAN PLANNING

The discipline of studying and planning new cities. Leonardo was both architect and planner, and devised an "ideal city" equipped with a full range of amenities. His scheme was to be realized in Vigevano, a splendid little town not far from Milan.

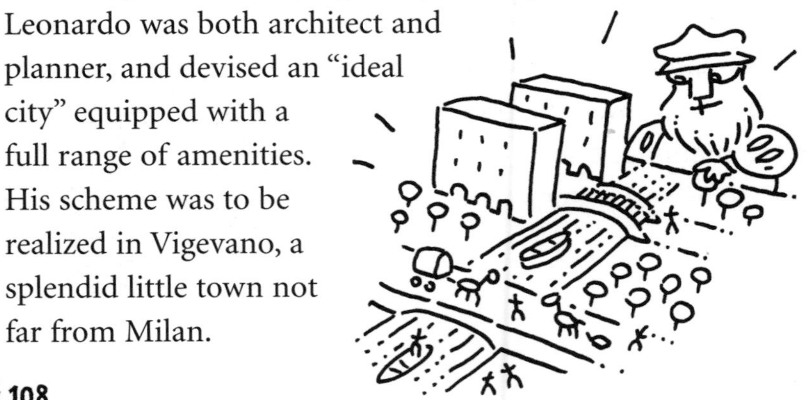

VITRUVIUS

An architect who lived and worked in ancient Rome. He was the author of the book *De architettura*, which was a source of inspiration and teaching for architects throughout the Renaissance, including Leonardo. The *Vivtruvian Man*, a figure inscribed in a circle and in a square, was drawn by Leonardo as an illustration for one of Vitruvius' works. Today the original drawing is preserved in the Gallerie dell'Accademia in Venice.

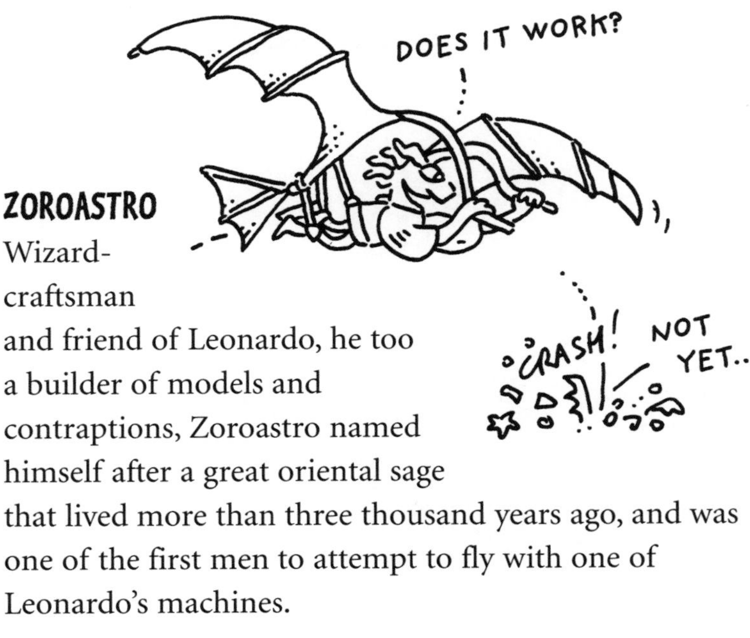

ZOROASTRO

Wizard-craftsman and friend of Leonardo, he too a builder of models and contraptions, Zoroastro named himself after a great oriental sage that lived more than three thousand years ago, and was one of the first men to attempt to fly with one of Leonardo's machines.

WWW.MUSEOSCIENZA.ORG

The website of Milan's Museo della Scienza, a museum dedicated to Leonardo. It contains working reconstructions of many of Leonardo's machines. On the site you can also find links to the websites of museums all over the world that house works of Leonardo.

LUCA NOVELLI

Writer and illustrator, he is the author of books about science and nature translated and published all over the world. He regularly collaborates with RAI (Italian state television) and as a journalist has directed the graphics and design magazine G&D for ten years.
He has won awards for best popular science author for children: Legambiente (2001), and the Andersen Award (2004).

More info, images and links about Luca Novelli and his books: www.lucanovelli.eu

FLASHES OF GENIUS

A series of biographies of great scientists—all written and illustrated by Luca Novelli—told in the first person.
The most fun and involving way to approach science and get to know the great minds that changed human history.
The series has been published in 20 languages.

FLASHES OF GENIUS

Einstein
and the Time Machine

Albert Einstein tells his story: as child he loves playing violin, but can't stand the discipline. Then his studies in physics, love, his job in the patent office and the first article on the theory of relativity. And then Nazism and his escape to the United States, where he will continue to study, publish, teach and fight for a world without war. In the meantime he becomes one of the most famous and respected figures on the planet. A fascinating story in which you will find the great scientist's curiosity, questions and humanity.

FLASHES OF GENIUS

Darwin
and the True Story of Dinosaurs

The life and discoveries of Charles Darwin, from his childhood in the English countryside hunting mice to his travels around the world as a passionate young naturalist, which will lead him to develop the theory of evolution and bring him worldwide fame. Including his journeys by horse through South America in search of new species, his study of the giant tortoises on the Galapagos, and his reserve in face of the heated polemics of his day; in sum the events, doubts, and passions of the life of the great naturalist.

FLASHES OF GENIUS

Galileo
and the First Star Wars

From learning to play the organ as a boy in Pisa to his old age, even in his blindness never losing the passion for research and dialogue with friends and students, this is the story of the life of Galileo Galilei, the father of modern science. He discovered the moon's mountains, Jupiter's satellites, and sunspots, and made a small fortune with his military compass. And then there is his encounter with the new ideas and techniques that were spreading throughout Europe, the clash with official doctrine, court life, the plague… a life of research, rigor and curiosity.

FLASHES OF GENIUS

Volta
and the Soul of Robots

Alessandro Volta's family wanted him to become a priest, but after seeing his success with the lightning rod they let him dedicate himself to electricity. He teaches at university, travels through Europe, and invents and discovers all kinds of things: the electroshock weapon, methane gas, the hydrogen lamp, electrometer, and his most famous invention, the battery. He achieved great fame in his lifetime; Napoleon himself will call him to Paris to demonstrate his discovery, which—a century later—would end up changing the world.

FLASHES OF GENIUS

Archimedes
and His War Machines

The life and adventures of Archimedes: his lessons in mathematics as a boy, on the beaches of Syracuse, his trip to Alexandria in Eygpt and his visit to its famed Library, his friendship with King Hiero and the war with Rome. And of course his many discoveries and inventions: the study of the principles behind the lever, the discovery of pi and the law of buoyancy (Eureka!). And above all the amazing contraptions and machines that made him legendary. The story, the creativity and the curiosity of a genius of Classical Greece.

FLASHES OF GENIUS

Mendel
and the Invasion of the GMOs

Gregor Mendel tells us about the two stages of his life: his childhood spent in the Bohemian countryside among flowers and sheep, and his time at the monastery, where he went to study natural science, biology, and herbal remedies. Nobody imagined that he would go on to become the father of modern genetics, thanks to his discovery of the laws of inheritance. After his success as a beekeeper, his famous experiments with peas in the convent's greenhouse, the meeting with Darwin that never took place… A life of perpetual curiosity, love of nature, and unending desire to improve the world.

FLASHES OF GENIUS

Hippocrates
Doctor at the Forefront

The son of a family of doctor-priests, Hippocrates was the first to set the foundations for scientific understanding of the human body and of diseases. To this day doctors take an oath to respect a moral code defined by Hippocrates. For these reasons he is considered the father of modern medicine. He traveled in Egypt, helped the Athens of Pericles to overcome the plague and was offered a position at the court of Artaxerxes, King of Persia. Despite his enormous fame, he remained full of questions. A figure of great humanitarian passion as relevant today as he was in his own time.

FLASHES OF GENIUS

Edison
How to Invent Everything and More...

The true story of Thomas Edison, the man who invented the future. As young man he sold newspapers aboard trains in order to be able to dedicate himself to his first great passion, chemistry. It was the beginning of a dazzling career as an inventor: he invented the phonograph, the first machine capable of recording and reproducing sounds, and shortly thereafter the light-bulb, the invention that would bring him worldwide fame. Then the first power station, the first sound film, the electric car… a life of research and faith in the power of science to improve life.

FLASHES OF GENIUS

Pythagoras
and the Cursed Number

Olympic champion, philosopher, music lover, and master mathematician. Pythagoras was all this and more: here is his life story, told by the man himself. His classes and lessons at the seaside as a child, with the sand as his chalkboard. His travels across the Mediterranean, his encounter with the ancient civilizations of the Near East and his great ideas: the reincarnation of all living beings, how numbers are the essence of all things. Up to the day of a frightening discovery: one of his students finds an infinite number, impossible to calculate…

FLASHES OF GENIUS

Newton
and the Formula for Antigravity

He was the head of the Royal Mint in London, attempted to turn lead into gold, and managed to avoid the black plague and the political turmoil of 17th-centruy England. And in the meantime Newton found the time to discover the law of universal gravitation, explain the tides and the movement of planets, decompose white light into the colours that compose it… And then there are his dealings with the great men of his time: Hooke, Huygens, Voltaire, and especially his despised rival Leibniz. The life of the genius in his own words, 84 years of never-ending study and insatiable curiosity.

FLASHES OF GENIUS

Lavoisier
and the Mystery of the Fifth Element

Antoine Lavoisier, the founding father of modern chemistry, was born in Paris in the middle of the 18th century. Though obliged by his father to be a lawyer, Lavoisier's true passion was for chemistry. Thus he became a tax collector by day, and brilliant scientist by night; he used his discoveries to improve the lives of everybody. From his experiments with air and discovery of oxygen and its role in how living organisms breathe, brought him immediate fame, up to his tragic end under the guillotine during the French Revolution. An intense life lived in the service of humanity and science.

FLASHES OF GENIUS

Magellan
and the Ocean that Wasn't There

He was the first man to sail all around the earth. He demonstrated with facts—and spices—that the world was round. He is the man who discovered the waterway linking the two greatest oceans of our planet, the first to reach the East by sailing to the West. This is his life, from his time as a page at the court of the King of Portugal to being the admiral of the first small but extraordinary fleet that dared to challenge the world's greatest ocean and the mysterious antipodes.

FLASHES OF GENIUS

Marie Curie
and the Atomic Secrets Revealed

An extraordinary young woman: brilliant, stubborn, passionate. As a student she decides to leave her beloved Poland to study at the Sorbonne, a decision that will change her life: in Paris she meets Pierre, her great love. Along with him she makes a momentous scientific discovery of radioactivity.
For her work she earns two Nobel prizes, and becomes the history's most famous woman scientist. The atom and the world, war and peace, nothing will be the same after her discoveries.

FLASHES OF GENIUS

Special Edition with DVD

THE LUMIÈRE BROTHERS

The brilliant Lumière brothers follow in their father's footsteps, a photographer with a penchant for inventions, and end up inventing the "moving image" or cinema: the most modern of the arts and one of the very symbols of the 20th century. Having grown up in the midst of shadow puppetry, magic lanterns, and photo studios, Auguste and Louis would build prototypes of film cameras by improving upon some of the strange contraptions that were popular at the time, such as the Kinetoscope and the photographic gun, and arrive at a revolutionary invention: the Cinematograph. A special colour edition, the book comes with a DVD and lots of advice from cinema masters for writing and shooting your own film.

BY THE SAME AUTHOR:

LA NOVELLINA

My First Science Dictionary

A for Atom, B for Biodiversity, C for Computer, D for DNA… Science uses so many words! From the pen of Luca Novelli, the author of the successful Flashes of Genius series, comes this dictionary of science that is accessible, illustrated and above all fun. A small pocket-sized encyclopaedia to learn about new concepts, go into more depth about essential topics or simply to flip through and discover random nuggets of science. With more than 300 pages, over 1000 definitions accompanied by entertaining colour illustrations.

WHAT
A STORY!